Christmas

COLORING BOOK FOR KIDS

FREE DOWNLOAD!

HOWDY PARENTS!

SIGN UP FOR OUR NEWSLETTER AND RECEIVE A FREE BONUS ACTIVITY BOOK PRINTABLE DIGITAL DOWNLOAD FOR YOUR KIDS.

SIGN UP HERE

http://freebies.papeteriebleu.com/pbkids

Manufactured by Amazon.ca
Bolton, ON

15827951R00042